PETER AND
F

Original story by Sergei Prokofiev
Retold by Michael Morpurgo
Series Advisor Professor Kimberley Reynolds
Illustrated by Joanna Carey

Letter from the Author

I first came across *Peter and the Wolf*, not in a story book or a picture book, nor in a play or a film, but through music. Many years ago, the great Russian composer, Sergei Prokofiev, set the story to music. It wasn't a musical, or an opera, simply a story told out loud – with music woven through it. It was a new kind of storytelling, musical storytelling, with different instruments, and different tunes, representing all the various characters: for Peter, the violins; for the wolf, the French horns; for Grandpa, the bassoon; for the duck, the oboe; for the bird, the flute; for the cat, the clarinet; for the hunters, the kettle drums. Prokofiev's wonderful *Peter and the Wolf* became so well known, so much loved, that like me, many cannot read the story without hearing that music in our heads.

So much did I love Prokofiev's *Peter and the Wolf*, that I now often perform musical and orchestral concert versions of my own stories: *The Mozart Question*, *The Pied Piper of Hamelin*, *On Angel Wings*, *Private Peaceful*, *War Horse*, *The Best Christmas in the World*, and *Where My Wellies Take Me*.

I owe a lot to that wolf, and Peter, and Prokofiev! I am a grandpa myself now, so I felt I would like to tell this story in a different way, as it had not been told before, from a grumpy old grandpa's point of view. So here it is. There's no music, I'm afraid, but there will be music in the words, I hope, and as you read it, you'll be picturing it in your head. It all happens in the Russian winter, deep in the forest, with snow all around. So put on thick socks, a warm hat, and curl up somewhere warm before you start!

Michael Morpurgo

I may be a grandpa now, but once upon a time I was a little boy myself. A long time ago now, but I was, and I don't forget. I especially don't forget the wolf.

I lived alone with my grandpa on the edge of a deep, dark forest. 'Walk off on your own into that forest, Peter,' he would tell me, 'and you'll get yourself lost, or worse still, eaten by wolves. It's a great wilderness. No one lives there. It goes on for ever and ever. Out there it is the wolves that

do the hunting. And do you know what wolves like to eat best? Us! You! Me! But most especially, little bony boys like you. So, never open the gate, Peter, you hear me? Don't you ever go out alone into that forest. Men like me, we are hunters, we have rifles. But even we never go out alone into the forest.'

He warned me so often, too often. Every time he did, it only made me long to open the gate and go out into that deep, dark forest – and on my own.

I'm not afraid, I told myself.
*I've climbed the big oak tree by
the wall and looked out over into the forest.
There's just lots of trees, and the meadow
and the pond,* I thought, *and birds, a rabbit
maybe sometimes, or a deer or two.*

But I've never seen a wolf. And what do I care about wolves anyway? I've seen lots of dogs in town, big ones too, and some of them look like wolves. I just clap my hands at them, shout at them, and they run off. What's a wolf to me? I'm not afraid of wolves.

I was the kind of boy who always thought I knew best. What did my silly, old, doddery grandpa know about anything?

It was one of those days – maybe once a week or so – when Grandpa went off hunting in the forest with his friends. He'd be gone all day. Every time, I would beg him to take me with him. But he never did. 'When you're older,' he said.

Why was it that everything I wanted to do had to wait till I was older? 'And besides,' he went on, 'it'll be too cold out there anyway. You stay here in the warm.'

It was true, it was cold – bitter cold.
There was snow on the ground – deep snow.
Everything was frozen, but I still wanted to go.

The last thing he said to me was the same as it always was: 'Now remember, Peter, when I'm gone, don't you dare open the gate. And don't go out into the forest, not even into the meadow, not even down to the pond. Like I told you, there are wolves out there and they eat boys, gobble them up and chew their bones.

'Stay inside in the warm and do your schoolwork like a good boy.' And off he went, with his rifle over his shoulder.

I hated being left behind, hated doing my schoolwork. What I liked to do best of all was to climb my oak tree by the wall, sit up there in the branches with the birds and look out over the meadow, over the pond on the edge of the forest. There were always ducks there and I especially liked watching the ducks.

So that morning, that's what I did. There I was, sitting high in the branches of my tree. With me up there, was Grandpa's ginger cat, who never stopped purring, and my little bird, a cackling laughing jay. Given half a chance, of course, the cat would eat the bird, and the bird knew it. One kept a wary eye on the other all the time.

Time and again, I told the cat, 'You can eat any bird you like, but not that one.' And time and again, I told the bird, 'Don't get too close to the cat.' And he'd look at me. 'Do you think I'm stupid?' his eyes would ask me. They were like brother and sister to me, both of them my best friends.

I had another best friend too, though. A duck. My duck. Other ducks came and went on the pond, but the only one who was always there was my duck. That was because she had a drooping wing, a wounded wing, and could not fly away with the others. So mostly she was left alone on the pond. She was there this morning. She was always hungry.

She quacked loudly at me from the frozen pond as soon as she saw me. I knew what she wanted. Grandpa would sometimes take me with him, out of the gate and down to the pond to feed her. So whenever she saw me, she thought I had food for her.

'I haven't got any bread. I can't feed you today,' I called down from high in the tree. 'I can't come down to the pond. I'm not allowed out on my own.'

But she went on quacking and quacking, swimming round and round excitedly in the middle of the pond, in the little circle of water she'd managed to keep clear of ice. I could see she was starving hungry. I had to feed her, and to do that, I would have to open the gate and go out into the meadow.

I remembered Grandpa's warnings. I knew that beyond the meadow and beyond the pond was the deep, dark forest, where the wolves lived, wolves that ate little boys and chewed their bones.

But that duck was my best friend – along with the bird and the cat. And anyway, I wasn't afraid, was I?

Quickly, I climbed down the tree and ran inside the house to fetch some bread from the kitchen.

Back outside, I opened the gate and walked out into the wide, white meadow, down towards the pond, the snow scrunching under my boots.

The duck quacked loudly at me as I came, slithering across the ice towards me. I crouched down at the edge of the pond to offer her the bread. She took it from my hand and swallowed it down, everything I gave her.

The bird flew down, cackling for some bread too. The cat was soon there too, eyeing the bird. 'No,' I told the cat firmly – I could see well enough what she had in mind. 'Have some bread instead,' I said. So I threw some bread crusts far out onto the snow for the cat and then dropped a few breadcrumbs at my feet for the bird – which did not please the duck, of course. *But you had to be fair,* I thought.

All of a sudden, a shiver went right through me, and I knew it wasn't the cold. The hair stood up on the back of my neck. The bird screeched and flew up into the branches of the tree. The cat was skittering off through the snow, yowling. Then still yowling, she was scrambling, scrabbling up the trunk of the tree. And all the while, the duck quacked loudly from the middle of the pond. But she wasn't quacking at me.

Something was moving at the edge of the forest. A wolf! A great, grey wolf was staring straight at me! His eyes yellow, his tongue red, his teeth sharp. I ran for it, stumbling through the snow. I could feel him coming after me – closer, closer.

I could hear the duck quacking angrily from the pond. I reached the gate, bolted it fast behind me and looked out. It was the duck that had saved me. The wolf was prowling round the pond, his eyes on the duck. This wolf preferred duck to boy, thank goodness!

He was licking his lips. He was testing the ice with his paw, and all the while the duck was quacking wildly at him from her circle of water in the middle of the pond, trying to flap her wings, trying to take off.

'Stay where you are!' I cried. 'Stay where you are!'

If only she had understood. If only she had listened! In her panic, she kept trying and trying to lift off and fly. But she couldn't fly. I knew she couldn't. She knew she couldn't. She got as far as the bank and crash-landed in the snow.

The wolf was bounding after her in a trice, racing round the lake. The duck was on her feet and half-running, half-flying, stumbling and tumbling, the wolf coming closer and closer all the time. Then he was on her. He had her. He swallowed her – whole.

One gulp and my duck was gone. He sat there now in the snow, staring at me, licking his lips. He was still hungry. Then, looking up, he caught sight of the cat and the bird high up in the tree, and came padding across the snow towards them.

He walked round and round the tree, his yellow eyes fixed on them, his red tongue hanging down, his teeth sharp, his tail waving high.
He had eaten one of my best friends. Now, he wanted the other two. As I watched, I felt the sadness inside me turning to anger, then anger growing into sudden courage.

It must have been his waving tail that gave me the idea – and his tail was, after all, the furthest away from those sharp teeth. All I needed for my plan to work was a rope – a long rope, a strong rope. I could tie a lasso in it and lower it down, wait for just the right moment. Then pull! Yes, it could work! I'd make it work!

There was a rope hanging in Grandpa's shed. I would do it! I would do it! I'd catch that wolf! I knew what to do. I raced across the yard to Grandpa's shed. Then, as quick as I could, I ran back over to the tree with it, crawling along the branch and out over the wall.

The wolf was prowling round the tree, snarling up at us. The bird flew down to be near me. He wanted to help. 'Fly down,' I told him, 'circle round his head, cackle at him, as witchily as you can. Make him giddy, make him mad.' And down he flew.

I turned to the cat. 'And you, hiss and yowl horribly at him, swipe your claws at him, make him madder still.'

Never had the cat hissed and yowled more horribly, never had the bird cackled more witchily.

As he flew round and round the wolf's head, the wolf was snapping and snarling, this way and that, in his fury and frustration. And all the while, I was making one end of the rope into a lasso and tying the other end around the branch beside me.

Then I was lowering the lasso, slowly, slowly, to the ground, and waiting, waiting, for the moment when the wolf would put his paw down in exactly the right place, inside the lasso, that lay close to him now, on the ground, a trap waiting just for him.

It took a while, a long, long while, and I was beginning to wonder whether I would ever catch him, whether he would ever put his paw in the right place. (The wrong place for him, of course!) But then he did, and I had him.

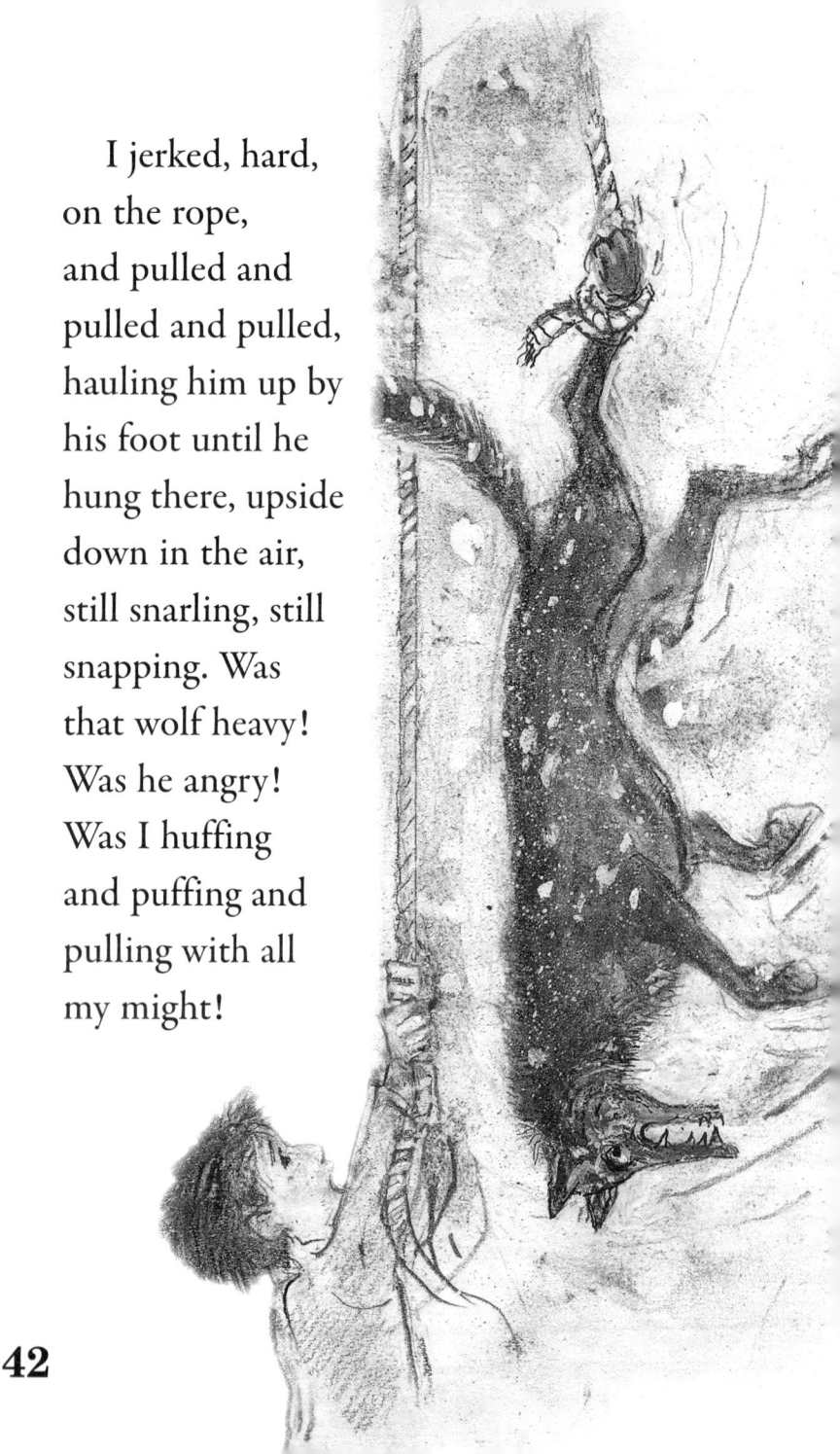

I jerked, hard, on the rope, and pulled and pulled and pulled, hauling him up by his foot until he hung there, upside down in the air, still snarling, still snapping. Was that wolf heavy! Was he angry! Was I huffing and puffing and pulling with all my might!

And was I happy to see him dangling there at last, helpless! We had done it! We caught him, the bird, the cat and me.

That was when Grandpa and the hunters came out of the forest, tracking the wolf's footprints. They had shot nothing.

We had caught a wolf, alive, and it was the biggest, angriest, snarliest wolf they had ever seen. They wanted to shoot him there and then.

'No!' I cried. 'He is our wolf. We have caught him, not you. So we say what happens to him. We say, let's take him to the zoo.'

You should have seen us all as we made our way into town that afternoon, Grandpa and me riding in the cart, with the wolf in the back, tied up in a net, still snarling and growling. And behind came the hunters, blowing their horns, and they were joined in time by drummers drumming and pipers piping. In the streets, the people clapped

and cheered, and I was the hero of the hour!
What a triumphant cavalcade it was! Even
the cat came with us, sitting on my lap and
purring happily. She had never in her life left
the house before, except to catch mice and
rats and birds. And the bird flew over her
head, not too close, cackling and laughing.
What fun! What joys!

But suddenly, in spite of all this, I felt sad. My duck, my dearest and best of friends, was not with us. I would never hear her quacking again. Then, even as I was thinking this, I heard her. She was still quacking. Was it from inside the wolf maybe? No, it was inside my head. She was alive. For me, she would always be alive. I would never forget her.

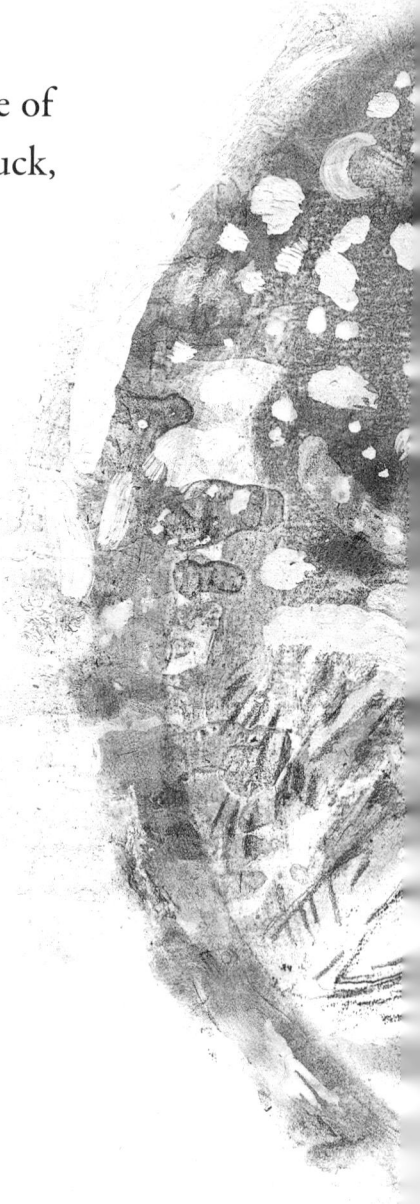

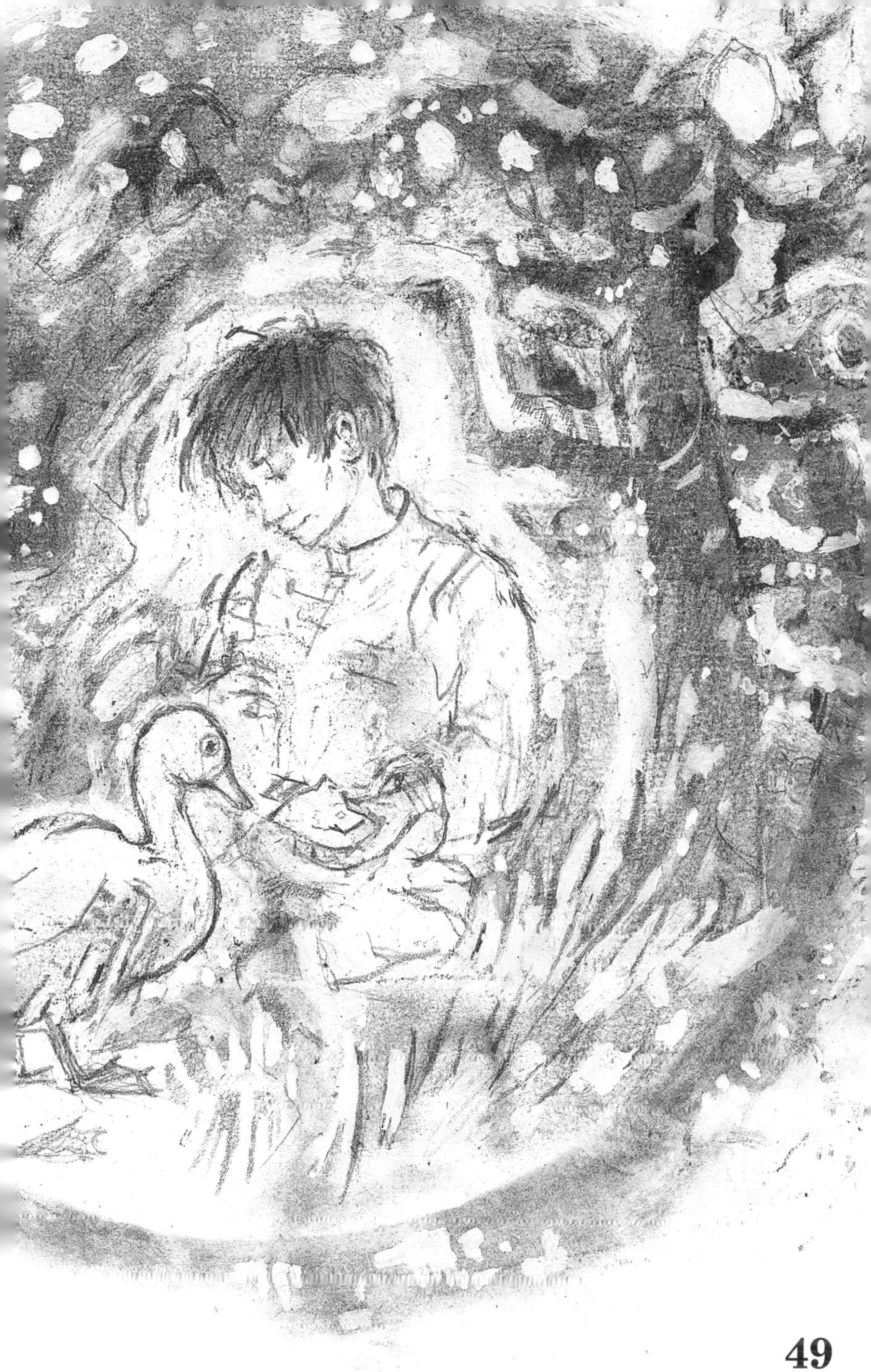

'You're a very naughty boy, Peter, going out through the gate like that, when I told you not to,' said Grandpa, grumpily. Then, with a smile, and a twinkle in his eye, he went on, 'But you're the best and bravest grandson a grandfather ever had, that's for sure.'

Peter and the Wolf: The Story and the Music

How it all began

Sergei Prokofiev was one of the most brilliant composers of the twentieth century. He was born in Russia in 1891. When he was only five, he astonished everyone with his amazing skill at playing and composing music. He wrote his first opera at the age of nine!

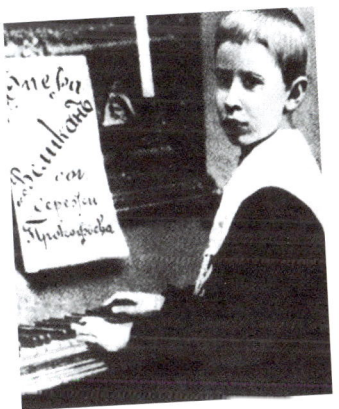

Prokofiev started learning the piano at the age of three.

Prokofiev was an amazing pianist, but he loved orchestral music best. Orchestral music is played by lots of different instruments working together.

Most orchestras include stringed instruments such as violins, violas and cellos; woodwind instruments such as flutes and clarinets; brass instruments like trumpets and trombones; and percussion instruments like drums and cymbals. When all these instruments play a piece of music together, it creates a wonderful rich sound.

The music can be loud or soft, peaceful or thunderous. It is full of emotion and colour!

By the time Prokofiev was in his forties, he was a very famous composer. He remembered how much he had loved music as a child, and he wanted to help other children to love it too. So he was very pleased when a theatre director in Moscow asked him to write a piece specially for children, combining words and music.

Sergei and the wolf

Prokofiev wanted to show children how the music could tell a story, and how each instrument had its own special voice. His big idea was to create a special musical story with lots of different characters. He would give each character its own orchestral instrument and its own theme tune. Unlike in an opera, the words wouldn't be sung. They would be spoken, so the story wouldn't get in the way of the music created by the instruments.

Prokofiev wanted the story to have lots of contrasts in it. That way, he could show the huge range of different sounds that orchestral music can make. So he thought of a wonderful story that included a tiny bird and a big, fierce wolf, along with lots of other contrasting characters.

All the characters had their own special instruments that helped to show how they moved and acted:

- The fast-moving little bird was played by the flute.
- The quacking duck was played by the oboe.
- The cat's tune was played by the clarinet.
- The big, scary wolf was played by the loud French horn.
- The hunters with their rifles were played by the drums.
- Slow-moving, deep-voiced Grandpa was played by the low bassoon.
- Peter's lively tune was played by all the strings in the orchestra – violin, viola, cello and double bass.

Prokofiev started work on *Peter and the Wolf* in 1935. He was so excited by the project that it only took him a fortnight to write all of the music and the words to go along with it. The first official performance was in 1936. Ever since then, it's been loved by generations of children – and adults!